HISTORIC
COMMUNITIES

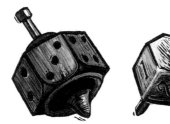

Games from long ago

Bobbie Kalman
Illustrations by Barbara Bedell

Crabtree Publishing Company

HISTORIC
COMMUNITIES

Created by Bobbie Kalman

For Tammy Everts

Editor-in-Chief
Bobbie Kalman

Writing team
Bobbie Kalman
David Schimpky
Tammy Everts

Managing editor
Lynda Hale

Editors
Tammy Everts
Petrina Gentile
Nelson Couto

Computer design
Lynda Hale

Special thanks to
Old Sturbridge Village, Upper Canada Village,
Mary Niman at the Detroit Antique Toy Museum

Separations and film
Dot 'n Line Image Inc.

Printer
Worzalla Publishing Company

Crabtree Publishing Company

350 Fifth Avenue
Suite 3308
New York
N.Y. 10118

360 York Road, RR 4
Niagara-on-the-Lake
Ontario, Canada
L0S 1J0

73 Lime Walk
Headington
Oxford OX3 7AD
United Kingdom

Cataloging in Publication Data
Kalman, Bobbie, 1947-
   Games from long ago

(Historic communities series)
Includes index.
ISBN 0-86505-482-7 (library bound) ISBN 0-86505-521-1 (pbk.)
This book examines the different types of games, including
outdoor games, parlor games, and board games, played by
children in nineteenth-century North America.

1. Games - History - 19th century - Juvenile literature. 2. Games -
Juvenile literature. I. Title. II. Series: Kalman, Bobbie, 1947- .
Historic communities.

GV1200.K35 1995   j790.1'922'09034   LC 95-3531
                                         CIP

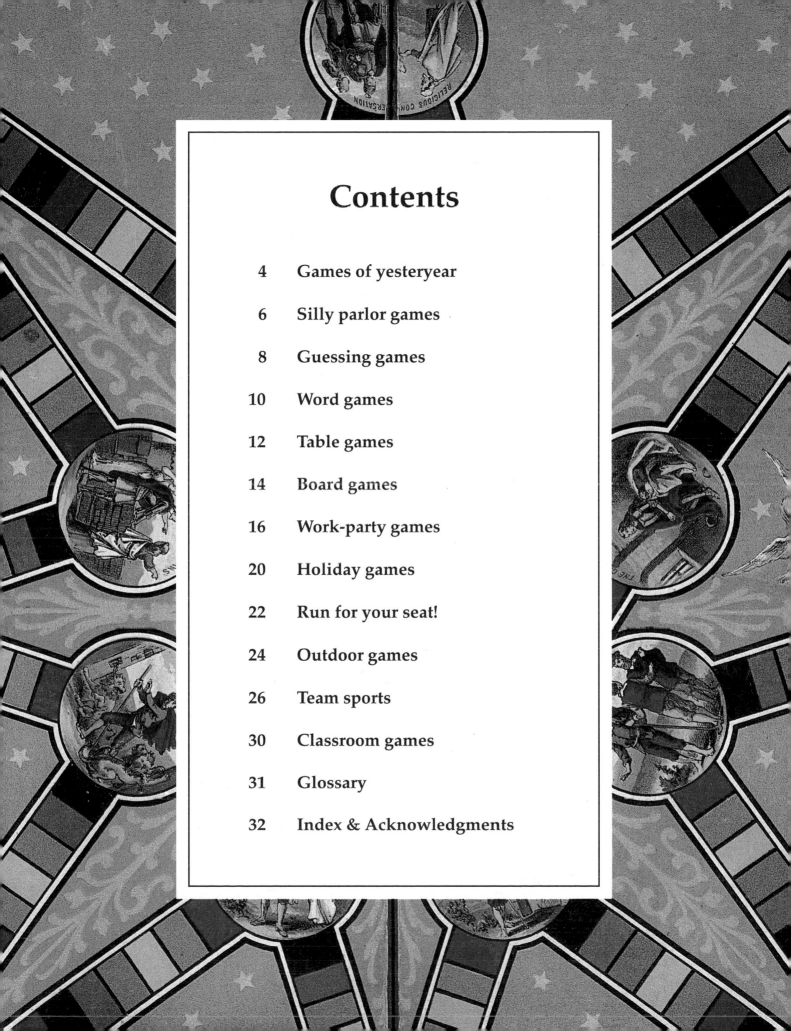

Contents

Games of yesteryear

Over a hundred years ago, there were no television sets, stereos, or video games, but there were always enough people around for playing games. Families were large—parents and several children, as well as an aunt, uncle, or a grandparent or two, lived under one roof. Children also played games at school, in the village, and at work parties.

Playing in the parlor

People who owned large homes often had a **parlor**. A parlor was a special room that was used for entertaining guests. When families invited neighbors to visit, they played games in their "best room." These games were known as **parlor games**. Parlor games often involved several people. Charades and Blind Man's Buff were popular parlor games. Guessing games, word games, and board games were also played in the parlor.

Children did not have many toys, so they invented games using their imagination and a few simple objects. How would you play this game?

4

Learned by word of mouth

Many of the games children play today are not learned from books. Children learn them from friends, who have learned them from other friends. Children have played the same games for almost two hundred years. You will recognize some of the games in this book, but a few old games may be new to you. Try them out with a group of friends. You can even come up with your own versions of old games. Design a board game or create a guessing game that uses modern people, places, and things.

This boy is showing his sister how to play the game of Gossip. You can learn how to play it by turning to page 17.

Silly parlor games

The main object of parlor games was to have fun. Sometimes the people watching the games had more fun than the people who were playing! The parlor games described on these two pages require no skill. Their only purpose is to make people laugh. Try them and see if you think they are funny.

The cudgel game

This game was a favorite among boys in the late 1800s. A **cudgel** is a stout club. Instead of real cudgels, the two blindfolded players are given rolled-up newspapers. They lie on their stomach, head to head, holding each other by the left hand. One player calls out "Are you ready?" When the other player replies "yes," the first player tries to swat him or her with the newspaper. Since the swatter is blindfolded, he or she usually misses. The other player then asks "Are you ready?" and tries to whack his or her friend. There is no point to this silly game, but it is fun to play and watch.

Playing the cudgel game is a good way to let off some steam. It is fun to watch the players miss their target and swat the floor.

Pinch, No Smiling

Pinch, No Smiling was a parlor game that tested self-control. To play Pinch, No Smiling, everyone sits in a circle. One by one, each player turns to a neighbor and pinches his or her nose. The first player to smile or laugh has to pay a **forfeit** such as jewelry or a favorite toy.

After everyone in the circle has been pinched, all the losers must "pay" to get their forfeits back. The wheeling and dealing is as much fun as playing the actual game! A player buys back his or her forfeit by performing a silly trick, such as acting like an animal, hopping around the room on one foot, or staying perfectly still and silent for a period of time. The winners of the game decide what the losers must do!

Is it a person? -no

Is it an animal? -no

Is it a place? -no

Is it an object? -yes

Would it fit in a room? -yes

Can it fit in your hand? -yes

Would you see it every day? -yes

Can you buy it in a store? -no

Is it made by people? -yes

Is it a toy? -no   Is it useful? -yes

Is it a common item? -yes

Would most people own it? -yes

Would children use it? -yes

Would women use it? -yes

Would men use it? -yes

Is it used in a house? -no

Is it used in a barn? -yes

Is it used on animals? -yes

Is it a horseshoe? -YES!

Guessing games

Parents encouraged their children to play guessing games because these games were good brain exercises! Charades and Twenty Questions are still played at parties today.

Charades

Charades is a fun game to play when people come to visit. Players take turns being the actor. Each player writes down a word, name, or phrase on a piece of paper and puts it in a hat. The first actor takes a piece of paper from the hat. He or she must act out the mystery word or phrase within one or two minutes. Sometimes the actor gives clues such as pulling on an ear, a gesture that means "sounds like," and then acts out a word that rhymes with the word on the paper. The player who guesses the word or phrase is the next actor.

Twenty Questions

The settlers loved to pass the time playing Twenty Questions. It is still a fun game. One person thinks of a person, place, or thing. The other players try to guess who or what it is by asking questions that can be answered "yes" or "no." For example, a player may be thinking of a blacksmith. If another player asks "Are you thinking of an animal?" the answer would be "no." If the next question is "Are you thinking of a person?" the player answers "yes." The game continues until the players discover who or what the person is thinking of or until twenty questions have been asked—whichever comes first.

Dumb Crambo

Two teams are needed for this game. Team 2 leaves the room while Team 1 picks a word, such as "pie," as well as a rhyming word to offer as a clue. Team 2 re-enters the room and is told that the secret word rhymes with "sky." Team 2's job is to act out the secret word. If the players on Team 2 are wrong, the Team 1 players hiss loudly. Team 2 keeps acting until the players guess the right word. Then it is Team 1's turn to leave the room while Team 2 picks a new word.

Games such as Charades and Dumb Crambo tested children's acting abilities. Can you guess what large gray animal this boy is pretending to be?

WORD GAMES

Games that involved letters and words helped children learn language skills. Even young children could play some word games once they knew the letters of the alphabet. Word games were popular with parents because they were educational and children were not rowdy while they played.

Would you put a queen inside your basket?

Is Cupid singing and flying as he is leaving?

I Have a Basket

To play this game, the players form a circle. The first player begins the game by saying "I have a basket." The person beside him or her asks "What's inside?" The first person has to name something that starts with the letter A. The second person has to name an object that begins with the letter B, and so on. The game gets interesting when the players reach the letters Q and X. What Q word would you put into your basket?

Cupid's Leaving

Cupid's Leaving is similar to I Have a Basket. To begin, all the players pick a letter, for example, S. The first player calls out "Cupid's leaving," and the next person asks "How?" The first person has to think of a word that starts with S and ends in "ing" to describe how Cupid is leaving. He or she might answer "singing." The second player then calls out "Cupid's leaving," and the third player asks "How?" The second player might say "sobbing." The game continues until someone is unable to think of an answer. The players then choose a new letter.

Anagrams

To play Anagrams, children used small squares of paper with letters of the alphabet written on one side. (You can use the tiles from a Scrabble game.) All the squares are placed face down on a table.

The players take turns turning over one square each. As soon as someone sees enough letters to make a word, he or she calls out the word and takes the letters. New letters are then turned over. If any of these can be added to an old word to make a new word, a person can call out the new word and "steal" the letters from the person who holds them. Players are also allowed to rearrange letters to make new words. Anagram players must think fast to hold on to their letters!

What new word could you make if the next letter were an E?

If you say "deer," you'll be out on your ear!

Taboo

Taboo players decide on a letter of the alphabet that will be forbidden in the game. One person is chosen to be It. The other players ask It questions that might force him or her to use the forbidden letter. For example, if the letter D were chosen, one player might ask "What animal has hoofs?" It would answer "a lamb." If It answered "deer," he or she would have used the forbidden letter. The questioning continues until It is forced to use the taboo letter. In a more difficult version of the game, the person who is It must answer in sentence form without using the taboo letter anywhere in the sentence: "The little lamb follows Mary to school on its four little hoofs."

Table games

Some table games required a steady hand or quick wit to win. In other games, victory depended on the luck of the draw.

Dominoes

Playing dominoes was a favorite pastime in the late 1800s. The game is still played today. Dominoes are flat, rectangular blocks called "tiles" or "bones." Each tile has two groups of dots on one side. The dots range in number from zero to six. Tiles with the same number of dots on both ends are called **doublets**.

One dominoes game is called Draw. The tiles are put in the middle of the table, face down. Each player draws three tiles and looks at them. The rest of the dominoes are left face down in the "boneyard." Whoever has the doublet with the most dots lays it on the table. The second player puts a domino with a matching number of dots against the doublet. Doublets are put down sideways, as shown on the left.

The next player must lay a match at the free end of a tile. If he or she cannot, the player must turn over new dominoes until a match is found. The first player to lay down all of his or her dominoes wins.

Tiddlywinks

Almost everyone has heard of tiddlywinks, but few people know how this game is actually played. Players use a disk called a **shooter** to flip smaller disks called **winks** into a cup that sits in the middle of the playing area. The object of the game is to be the first player to sink all of his or her disks into the cup. In the past, players took this game very seriously and practiced flipping winks in their spare time.

Pick-up sticks

Pick-up sticks, or **jackstraws**, was a very popular game among North American settlers. To play, all that was needed was a pile of wood splinters or straws. Some fancy pick-up-stick games had ivory "straws." Modern versions of jackstraws use wooden or plastic sticks. The sticks are heaped in the middle of a table. Each player takes a turn removing one stick from the pile. The challenge is to do so without moving any of the other sticks.

Cards

In the early 1800s, most children's card games were designed to be educational. Card games helped children learn about math, geography, history, and science. Some card games even taught girls about cooking.

In the 1850s, people began to play card games for fun. Decks of cards were very colorful. Our Birds, Old Maid and Old Bachelor, and Dr. Busby were lively card games. Parents did not allow their children to play with regular playing cards because they did not want to encourage gambling.

The card game Our Birds taught about the birds of North America.

Today, the game of Old Maid and Old Bachelor is called Old Maid.

Dr. Busby was invented in the United States, but it quickly became popular in Europe.

Board games

Some of the board games the settlers played had been around for centuries. Chess, checkers, and backgammon are examples of old favorites, but many new board games were also created in the 1800s. Some helped players learn about history, geography, or science. Others taught children the value of working hard and behaving well.

The value of hard work

Errand Boy was a popular board game in the 1800s. This game, which is shown on these pages, tried to show children the value of hard work and good deeds. Using a **teetotum** to determine how far to move on the board, players followed the career of an errand boy as he was promoted in the company.

Players who landed on squares describing hard work and good behavior could move ahead. Players who landed on squares that described dishonest acts or laziness had to move back or go to jail. The winner was the player who became the president of the company!

The board game squares (reading as shown):

19 | THEFT 18 GO TO PRISON

GRITY 20 GO TO 21. | DISHONEST 17 GO BACK TO 8 | INATTENTION 16 LOSE ONE TURN

PRISON GO BACK TO BEGINNING AND START ANEW.

PROMOTED TO SALESMAN 23 EXTRA TURN | 15

2 | 24 | 25 | ACCURACY 14 | 13

GAMBLING 26 GO BACK TO 13 | DISCIPLINE 12 BACK TO 10

28 | 27 | POLITENESS 11 GO TO ACCURACY 14

NEGLECT OF BUSINESS 29 GO BACK TO 19 | 10

30 | LAZINESS 9 GO BACK TO 4

32 | ABILITY 31 GO ON TO MANAGER 34 | 8

3 ND | 33 | CONFIDENCE 7 GO TO 10.

TH 000 2 | DRUNKENESS 35 GO BACK TO 24 | MANAGER 34 | ENGAGED 4 EXTRA TURN | 5 | HONESTY 6 GO TO 11

36 | DULLNESS 3 GO BACK TO NO.1.

HA 000 | FRAUD 37 GO TO PRISON | 2

HEAD OF FIRM 38 | START. 1

APPLICATION OFFICE

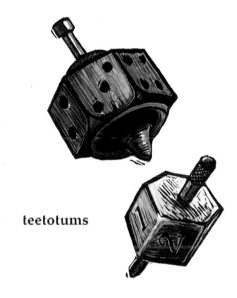

teetotums

In most board games, players moved pieces across squares on a board. To determine how many moves they could make, they spun a teetotum (above) or a number disk (below). Many people did not use dice because dice were associated with gambling.

Work-party games

Whenever there was a big task such as raising a barn or making apple cider, the settlers organized a work party called a **bee**. There were bees for husking corn, making quilts, and harvesting crops. Children often took part in the work or joined in the party afterwards. A big part of the bee was feasting, dancing, and playing games. Playing games made the work seem like fun.

A-mazing!

During the harvest, parents sometimes set up a maze of hay sheaves to keep their children occupied. The children wandered through the maze or played hiding games. While the children played, the parents had a chance to get work done or gossip with other adults. Mazes kept children amazed for hours!

Gossip

The first settlers did not have newspapers to tell them what was happening in the world. When people gathered at a bee, they exchanged news and information. Sometimes the news changed as it traveled.

The game of Gossip shows how the details of a news story change when the story passes from person to person to person. One player whispers a sentence in another player's ear. The sentence might be "Susan gave her itchy cat a bath. The bubbles made her father sneeze." The person who receives the message whispers it to the next person; however, the message is now "Susan gave her filthy cat to Ralph. The puddles gave her darker knees." As the message is passed along, more mistakes are made. The final message might be "Susan had a silky rat. She laughed because its riddles gave her fleas!"

In the game of Gossip, people learned not to trust their ears. How could the phrase "Susan gave her itchy cat a bath" change to "Susan gave her filthy cat to Ralph?"

Apple games

After the autumn apple harvest, the settlers gathered to peel the apples and string them up to dry. The dried fruit could be eaten throughout the winter. Games played at these bees involved—you guessed it—apples!

One apple game was believed to predict the future! A person pares an apple, leaving the peel in one long, winding piece, closes his or her eyes, and tosses the peel. The peel falls to the floor in a shape that resembles a letter of the alphabet. The letter just might be the first initial of the person the thrower will marry!

Did you know that apples float? To play Bobbing for Apples, float some apples in a tub of water. Players put their hands behind their back. Then everyone tries to remove an apple from the tub with his or her teeth. This is more difficult than it sounds! The apples bob and bounce out of reach at the slightest touch.

To play the game of Snap Apple, hang an apple from the ceiling with a string. Try to take a bite of it as it swings. No hands allowed!

18

Corn husking

After the harvest, everyone gathered to husk corn for winter storage. The young man who found a red ear of corn was allowed to kiss the young woman sitting closest to him. Some men cheated by bringing red corn to the bee in their pockets. Not all girls were happy when a young man produced an ear of colored corn!

Holiday games

Holidays provided a chance for settlers to get together. They looked forward to special days such as Christmas, Valentine's Day, Thanksgiving, and Hallowe'en. Get-togethers usually meant lots of food and fun games!

Bag and Stick

The game of Bag and Stick was popular at Christmas parties in the late 1800s. A paper bag filled with treats is hung from the ceiling. One person is blindfolded, spun around, and given a stick. The person is allowed a certain number of tries at hitting the bag with the stick. Each person takes a turn until the bag is finally broken. Everyone scrambles to grab the goodies.

Famous Romances

The game of Famous Romances was popular at Valentine's Day parties. Each player has a heart stuck to his or her back. The player does not know what name is on his or her heart, only that it is part of a famous couple. This game is played like Twenty Questions. Each person must first find out his or her identity by asking the other players questions that can be answered with a yes or no. "Am I a man?" "Am I still alive?" "Is my partner a king?" The next step is to locate the partner. Examples of famous couples are Adam and Eve and Anthony and Cleopatra. Fictional couples such as Superman and Lois Lane or Beauty and the Beast can also be used to play the game.

(left) The Bag and Stick game is similar to the Mexican tradition of breaking a piñata on birthdays and at Christmastime.

The Cobweb Game

The Cobweb Game was popular at Christmas parties. A beautiful spider made of wire and other materials hung from the ceiling. Long pieces of string or ribbon—one for each player— were attached to the spider, then wound around the room in a tangled web. The strings reached under the furniture, through doors, and even up and down stairs! The object of the game was to follow one piece of string from the spider to the end, where a Christmas present was waiting.

The Cobweb Game was the highlight of many Christmas parties. In some homes, the spider and its colorful ribbons were used as the main Christmas decoration, instead of a tree!

Run for your seat!

Children today have loads of energy. The children of the past were no different. They enjoyed games that allowed them to run and compete with one another. The games on these pages are similar to Musical Chairs. They require children to run for their seats!

Spin the Trencher

Many settler families owned large wooden **trenchers**. Trenchers were long shallow dishes that were used for preparing or serving food. Trenchers also had another purpose—they were used for playing Spin the Trencher. You can use a large plastic bowl when you play Spin the Trencher.

The bowl is put on the floor, and the players sit in a circle around it. Each player chooses the name of an animal. One player is It. He or she spins the bowl and calls out the name of one of the animals, such as "woodchuck." The player who is the woodchuck has to run to the bowl and keep it spinning. As the woodchuck gets up, the person who is It takes his or her spot. Now the woodchuck is It. If a player allows the bowl to stop spinning, he or she is out of the game.

Post Office

In this game, each player chooses the name of a city. One player is the postal clerk. The rest of the players sit in a circle. The clerk calls out "The mail is going from Chicago to Toronto" (or any other two cities). The players who chose those cities have to exchange seats without letting the postal clerk steal either of their seats.

This woodchuck lost his seat and decided to sit in the trencher instead of spinning it.

In settler days, the mail was delivered by stagecoach, boat, or train. In this picture, the postal clerk's daughter waits for the train to pick up the mailbag.

Duck, Duck, Goose

This game is still very popular. All players sit in a circle, except the player who is It. He or she walks around the outside of the circle and touches each player's head, saying "duck." After calling out "duck" a few times, It suddenly calls out "goose." The player who is the goose has to jump up and chase It around the circle. If It runs around the circle and sits in the goose's spot without being tagged, the goose becomes It.

Being chased by a wild goose was a good reason to run fast!

Outdoor games

Although boys and girls played many of the same games indoors, they often played different games outside. Boys did not take part in clapping, skipping, or string games. Girls were not included in team sports or contests such as tug-of-war.

Battledore and Shuttlecock

This game is an early version of badminton. The **battledore** is the racket, and the **shuttlecock** is the birdie. The goal of the game is to keep the shuttlecock in the air as long as possible.

Graces

The game of Graces was played by two players, either two girls or a girl and a boy. Boys did not play Graces with one another because it was considered a "girl's game." Each player had a stick. Using the sticks, the players tossed a hoop to one another. The game was meant to encourage children to move gracefully.

Ring Taw

The most popular marble game in settler times was called Ring Taw. You can play this game today. Draw a large ring on the ground. Draw a smaller circle inside it and place several small marbles, called **nibs**, in the circle. The players crouch outside the large ring. From there, each player takes a turn flicking a large marble, called a **shooter**, into the circle. The goal is to knock other marbles out of the circle. Each player keeps the marbles he or she knocks out. The winner is the player with the most marbles.

Boys and girls of all ages enjoyed a rousing game of Battledore and Shuttlecock.

It is easy to toss a hoop when playing Graces, but catching the hoop is much more challenging.

Team sports

Some outdoor games were rough—even dangerous! There was always a winner and a loser. The goal was to show which boy was the strongest and bravest. Girls were seldom allowed to participate. Parents believed that rough play was "unladylike."

Tug-of-war

Tug-of-war was not really a war, but it was still a pretty tough game! Two teams were formed, and a line was drawn on the ground between them. The teams held on to a thick rope and pulled with all their might. The goal was to pull the other team across the line. Participants had to have strength, endurance, and very strong arms!

The game called Americans and English was similar to tug-of-war. Instead of using a rope, each team selected a leader. The two leaders locked arms. The team members held on to each other and to their leader, and tried to pull the other team across the line.

In tug-of-war, the goal was to pull the opposing team over a line. Sometimes children played tug-of-war with a stream or mud puddle between the two teams. The losing team landed right in the water or mud. The threat of getting wet or muddy added a bit more excitement to the game.

Shinny

Shinny was a popular boy's game. It was similar to ice hockey but was played in open fields or on empty lots. Each player had a stick and used it to hit a small ball into a goal area. Most children used tree branches for sticks and everything from a ball of yarn to a crushed tin can for a ball. In some places, organized shinny teams hit leather balls with well-made sticks.

A fast-paced game of shinny was a favorite pastime for energetic boys.

Lacrosse

Settlers learned the game of lacrosse from the Native people, who played it long before Europeans settled in North America. Lacrosse is still very popular, especially in Canada. A lacrosse stick is long and has a net at one end. It is used to catch and fling the ball into a goal area.

Football

Modern North American football is actually a combination of two older sports—soccer and rugby. In the 1800s, football was similar to modern-day soccer. According to the rules, the team that scored two out of three times was the winner. In the 1870s, university football teams had rules that allowed players to carry the ball. Defenders tackled anyone carrying the ball so they couldn't take it across the goal line. These new rules made football the game it is today.

Lacrosse players move quickly to score goals, but football players rush to avoid being tackled.

Baseball

In the mid-1800s, baseball became a popular sport in the United States. Professional teams played in cities throughout the country. It was also a favorite pastime for many boys. The rules haven't changed much since the 1800s, but there are a few differences. In the past, the batter was called a **striker** or a **batsman**, and he could hit the ball in a variety of ways. Some batsmen hit the ball over their head, whereas others hit the ball on the ground, similar to the way a golf ball is hit. The bat was often homemade—sometimes it was just a big stick! Players did not wear helmets or even baseball gloves!

Over a hundred years ago, baseball was played much as it is today, but without modern equipment. As the batter prepares to hit the ball, the catcher is ready to catch it—with his bare hands!

Classroom games

Classroom games made learning more fun. Some were played at any time, whereas others were reserved for Friday afternoons.

Buzz

The game of Buzz showed how well children knew their numbers and multiplication tables. Everyone sits in a circle and begins to count in turn. When the number seven, a number with seven in it, or a multiple of seven comes up, the player must say "buzz" instead of the number. For example, the count around the circle would go like this: "One...two...three...four...five...six... buzz...eight...nine...ten...eleven...twelve... thirteen...buzz...fifteen...sixteen...buzz...eighteen..."

If a player does not say "buzz" at the proper time, he or she is out of the game. The counting continues until only one player is left.

Spelling bee

Spelling bees were popular in settler times. A week of classes often ended with a spelling bee on Friday afternoon. On winter evenings adults held spelling bees of their own.

The class divides into two teams that line up along opposite walls of the classroom. The teacher gives a word to one team member. If that person cannot spell the word correctly, he or she sits down and is now out of the game. Then the word is given to a player on the opposite team. The game continues with new words until only one player is left.

Alphabet Geography is a real brainteaser! One person names a city, country, or continent— "France," for example. The next player has to name a place that starts with the last letter in "France," so he or she might say "England." The player after that might say "Detroit." Can you think of a place name that starts with T?

30

Glossary

anagram A word that is made by rearranging the letters of another word, such as "saw" and "was"

batsman An early name for the batter in baseball

battledore The racket used to hit a shuttlecock in an early version of badminton

bee A gathering of people to do work, such as raising a barn or harvesting crops

blacksmith An artisan who makes things out of iron

cudgel A short, thick club or stick; also the act of hitting someone with a cudgel

Cupid The Roman god of love who shot people with arrows of love. Cupid was usually pictured as a baby angel.

doublet A domino tile that has the same number of dots on each end

errand A small job or duty

forfeit Something given or taken away as a punishment for losing a game

gossip Stories and news passed from person to person, often containing mistakes or lies

husk The rough outside covering of an ear of corn

jackstraws Sticks made of wood or plastic, used in playing pick-up sticks

lacrosse A traditional Native game played with a ball and long sticks that have a net on the end

nib A small marble used in Ring Taw

pare To remove the peel from an apple or other fruit or vegetable

parlor A special room in which guests were entertained and games were played

postal clerk A person whose job is to make sure that letters and packages are delivered

sheaf A bundle of hay or grain

shinny A game similar to field hockey that is played with sticks and a small ball

shooter A disk used to flip smaller disks into a cup in a game of Tiddlywinks; also, the large marble used to knock out the nibs in Ring Taw

shuttlecock The object that is kept in the air in a game of badminton

striker An old name for the batter in baseball

taboo Something that is forbidden or disliked

teetotum A spinning top with numbers that can be used in games instead of dice

tile A domino piece

trencher A long shallow dish used for preparing or serving food

wink A small disk used in playing tiddlywinks

woodchuck A small furry animal, also known as a groundhog

Index

Acknowledgments

Illustrations and colorizations
All illustrations by Barbara Bedell
    except the following:
Allan and Deborah Drew-Brook-
    Cormack: page 18 (top, bottom right)
Sarah Pallek: title page, pages 13, 15
David Schimpky: page 22

Photographs
Marc Crabtree: title page, pages 3, 14-15
Thomas Neill/Old Sturbridge Village:
    page 24

5 6 7 8 9 0 Printed in the U.S.A. 4 3 2 1 0 9 8 7